With Very best!

Sandra

S. Barnett

ISBN 0 9535617 3 9

Inspirations

By
Sandra Barnett

Published by
TROPIC PUBLICATION
P.O.Box 5786 Leicester UK.

Printed in Lebanon by
PRINTING GROUP
P.O.Box 5687/13 Beirut, Lebanon

Project editor
Hajra Makda

Dedicated to

Paul Barnett & Eynon Thomas

CONTENTS

Wooded Walk	1
Babies	2
Winter	4
Fishing	5
Weddings	6
The dentist	7
The River Avon	9
The River Severn	10
The scarecrow	12
Spring	13
Beach Walk	14
The Little Doll	16
Good old Days	18
Television	20
The Gnome	21
Sophie	22
Parchute Jump	23
Gloomy day	25
Canal Walk	26
The Lonely Christmas Tree	27

The Fairground   28

Brean Sands   30

Scarborough View   31

Bonfire night   32

Reminiscing   33

Newly Weds , Son   34

Memories   35

Little girl, Friend   36

Someone special, My Love   37

Both of you   38

Mum, Grandad   39

Nan, Wishes   40

The Zoo   41

The evening Sky   43

The Great Central Park   44

Children's Parties   45

Motorways   46

Time on Mars   48

Summer   49

Autumn   50

Into the depth of a shady wood
A glimpse of a deer as it calmly stood
I approach very slowly, trying not to scare
He's very cunning and knows I'm there
His eyes are fixed and watching me
Then dashes behind a nearby tree
Off into the thick dense bushes he goes
Where nobody treads and no one knows
A sea of bluebells all around
And broken branches on the ground
The rustle of leaves beneath my feet
A log for a table, with a wooden seat
Squirrels scurrying really fast
They hear my steps as I walk past
It's really beautiful walking under the trees
With a shimmer of sun, and a light cool breeze
The different sounds from the birds I hear
I wait and see if they appear
They're out of sight, too far for me
Only a flutter of wings I see

A lovely butterfly on dog-rose petals
Between the bushes and stinging nettles
An old tree stump where the fungus grows
And colored berries amongst hedgerows
Pinecones scattered here and there
The woody perfume fills the air
I'm near the end of my nature trail
As I see a fox with his bushy tail
Scooting along he's gone to roam
No doubt he'll be back, when I've gone home
It's a lovely walk in the woods like this
All peaceful and quiet, full of heavenly bliss.

BABIES

A new born baby, a bundle of joy
With all the same needs, for a girl or boy
Cute and cuddly just lying there
Without any problems, worries or care
Wrapped all up in their little cot

All cozie and warm, this tiny tot
Then they awake, they want their feed
You have to be there, whatever they need
Then the baby starts crying, and not very happy
Lying uncomfortable, with a very wet nappy
The nappy needs changing, that's not much fun
When it's all dripping wet, and starting to run
Washed and dressed in nice romper suit
And fast asleep they look so cute
During the night, you're all restful and calm
You hear a cry from the baby alarm
Another night without any sleep
And baby clothes all in a heap
The extra hours of chores you spend
Your baby's needs, you have to attend
The moments of joy, and all that pleasure
Those golden moments you'll always treasure
That's the part of becoming a mother
Another few years, you'll have another.

Winter again, the nights draw near
Early dark evenings most people fear
Trees and hedges all cold and bare
Frost on the ground and a nip in the air
Coats and hats with gloves to match
The colds and flu that people catch
Freezing cold with ice and snow
People indoors with fires aglow
Lakes and ponds the ice will lay
A dangerous place where children play
Holly with berries a lovely bright red
Children out playing upon their sled
Prints in the snow what a robins made
And darker nights are starting to fade
There's still a few months of winds and rain
Before it comes round to spring again
Beautiful snowdrops starting to form
The weathers changing and getting warm
Birds are back; you can hear them sing
Winters over, it's nearly spring.

FISHING

Alongside the canal I slowly plod
With tackle in basket and carrying my rod
Passing by men on a fishing match
Keep nets ready for the fish they catch
I find a spot just right for me
Just under a hanging willow tree
All set and ready I've cast my float
When comes along a narrow boat
Splashing the water floats bobbing about
I have to give up and pull it out
Anxiously waiting as the boat goes by
Then cast out again for another try
Sitting and waiting and watching the float
I hear the sound of another boat
Again I sit and anxiously wait
As I prepare my hook with maggots for bait
Casting out again I try in vain
When down it comes the heavy rain
So up it goes my fishing brolly
As the bailiff appears all smiles and jolly

Caught any fish he asks with a glance
It's been that busy I haven't had chance
Sitting under my brolly I try again
Listening to the sound of the pouring rain
They're all packing up from the fishing match
Are there any fish here for me to catch?
There's no one left they've gone away
I think I'll come back another day.

WEDDINGS

There's a lot to planning a wedding day
All those decisions, and expenses to pay
Choosing the church and reception hall
For a lovely big wedding, or will it be small?
What sort of transport? There's so much choice
From a horse drawn carriage, to a white Rolls Royce
A photograph album to keep and treasure
Bridesmaids dresses all made to measure

A flowing brides dress full of lace that trails
The groom and best man to wear top hat and tails
A beautiful bouquet in colours to match
To throw away, for someone to catch
Choosing the cake and how many tiers
The bottom layer you keep for years
A cold buffet or a sit down roast
Champagne or sherry for people to toast
Disc jockey playing music, or a local band
For the bride and groom to dance hand in hand
Whatever you choose, no matter what people say
Always remember, it's your special day.

 THE DENTIST

Six monthly appointments, don't they come quick
The thought of going can make people sick
Anxiously waiting, the time ticking by
Twiddling your thumbs, cos your nerves are all high

You look at a book, but can't keep it still
For wondering what tooth he'll take out, or fill
Or a scale and polish, you hope that's all
When you here a voice, it's your name they call
You anxiously sit in the big black chair
Looking up to the ceiling, you gaze and stare
Approached by the dentist, wearing gloves and mask
"Had any problems, they always ask
Open wide while I take a look
While holding a mirror and pointed hook
The digging and poking, they go to town
While the nurse sits listening and writing things down
'There's a little hole here where I tap
So a scale and polish, and fill the gap
Just a small needle into the gum
"I'll scale and polish, while it's going numb
The noise of the drill as it whizzes around
Whistling and screeching, 'oh what a sound
You rinse out your mouth all wobbly and funny
There's bits everywhere, the drink warm and runny
All down your chin, cos you can't feel your face
With your crooked smile, you feel a disgrace
Trying not to smile, as to let people know

You hurry to pay, cos your anxious to go
Now it's all over, you don't really care
It's another six months till you go back there.

———∿∿∿———

THE RIVER AVON

The river Avon, it's not far from me
Where I like to stroll before my tea
Time for myself and without a care
Just walking the dog and going nowhere
It's a lovely place to bring a child
But the grass is long and really wild
The river's quite clear and flowing fast
There's flies all around, as I walk past
It's very windy with a huge big black cloud
I hear children playing, they're shouting out loud
It feels rather chilly; it's starting to rain
Over in the distance, the sound of a train
In the middle of a field, there's some ducks in a pond

With a lovely big farmhouse a little further beyond
Standing here on a bridge, my dog and me
Looking down on the water, a small fish I can see
The cows are approaching, they're watching us two
There's not many of them, only a few
The dog's getting tired, so we're now on our way
No doubt we'll return, the very next day.

 RIVER SEVERN

The river Severn runs fast and wide
With nooks and crannies for fish to hide
Deep embankments with nice wide ledge
All nicely sheltered with a bushy hedge
A large tree stump just feet away
The ideal spot for me to stay
Sitting all comfortable, and set up at last
With rod prepared and ready to cast
Feeder filled up with plenty of bait

Now it's time to sit and wait
After a while, looking into the river
A glimpse of my rod, just starting to quiver
Lifting my rod the line goes all-tight
I've caught a barbel, he's starting to fight
Down the river, just like a steam train
Gripping tight to the rod, I find it a strain
With the rod in hand, it goes with a thump
As I fall down the bank, and over the stump
Leaning over the water, full frontal I lay
While holding on tight, the fish gets away
Back to my seat, clutching my rod and reel
I can't believe how shattered I feel
Sitting relaxing for a moment of leisure
Just sitting by water, brings me so much pleasure
So many nice spots to sit on the Severn
No hustle and bustle, just peaceful and heaven.

My body made up, from rags and straw
Perched on a fence, not touching the floor
A little old hat, and made up face
With arms and legs, stretched out in place
In the middle of a field, in the open air
Out in the country, with no worries or care
Sitting out here, and enjoying the view
No work to go to, and nothing to do
Out in the distance, what a beautiful site
There's a lovely farmhouse, across to my right
A glimpse of a lady on a lovely white horse
Galloping round, on an obstacle course
The farmers out gathering all of his sheep
While the cows on my left, all having a sleep
A large flock of birds have flown down from a tree
They're looking for food; they're not scared of me
I'm happy here on this lovely old farm
Amongst all my friends, all peaceful and calm
Except for the night, all alone in the dark
When I just hear the sound of the farmers dog bark

There's no lights at all, only stars in the sky
Or the odd car in the distance, as it passes by
Just a matter of time, for the end of nightfall
Dawn will break, and the cockerel will call
Animals and birds in the field I will share
To them I'm not scary, but I don't really care
The birds walk all over me, they don't live in fear
They all keep me company, I'm really happy here.

SPRING

Tulips and daffodils spring time is here
Buds on trees and bushes appear
Lighter evenings and brighter days
Cows in the fields all out to graze
Lambs being born this time of year'
Newborn calves and fields with deer
Easter chicks how cute they look
Little rabbits, and a baby duck

Baby birds just learning to fly
The sun peering through the lovely blue sky
Squirrels return for their daily feed
Pinching the nuts, and wild birdseed
Summer outfits in all the shops
Bright colored shorts and fancy tops
People booking their holiday trips
On coaches and planes or cruising ships
A beautiful time with summer ahead
When you hear birds singing while lying in bed
But if it's bright sunshine, in bed we don't stay
We all make the most, of a beautiful day.

BEACH WALK.

Strolling along on the lovely soft sand
Carrying my sandals in my hand
The gentle warm breeze flowing through my hair
As I watch the seagulls in the air

The glare on the sea from the bright golden sun
There's children playing, and having fun
Running around, they scream and shout
While waves are rolling in and out
Horses and donkeys, there on the beach
An ice cream van, in easy reach
Sucking a lolly, a nice cool treat
As I feel the waves around my feet
Passing sand castles on top of a mound
And people sunbathing all around
I have a rest, on top of a hill
The air is warm and very still
A nice cool treat again I yearn
I'd better go back before I burn.

I'm a little doll, in a shop for sale.
I'd be sitting on top of a shelf,
all neat for people to see
Along then comes a family,
with a sweet and innocent girl
They're walking over towards me,
her heads all in a whirl
She's turning around excited,
looking up at all the rest
But chooses me above them,
cos I must be the best
She picks me up and holds me,
then carries me away
Off to her house I'm taken,
that's where I'm going to stay
My clothes are taken off me;
she starts to comb my hair
I've got no socks and shoes on;
I'm freezing cold and bare
I'm thrown into a doll's pram
with lots of other toys

Down to the park we're going,
  with other girls and boys
On all the swings they put me,
  they throw me all around
I wish they could have left me,
  in the place where I was found
Back home they're sitting watching,
  their programs on the telly
While the girls just sitting drawing,
  all over my bare belly
She's started pulling my hair,
  and my eyes are poked right out
And because I'm only a doll,
  I can't cry, scream or shout
I'm thrown into a toy box,
  in a heap with all the rest
I thought I was specially chosen,
  cos I was liked the best
It's gone all dark and squashed now,
  the lids put on the top
I wish I was on the shelf again,
  in the little toyshop.

Those bygone days when times were hard
No cooking oil, just pounds of lard
Things for granted you never took
Cos all you had was a ration book
Not the way we live today
Easy to get things, however you pay
Hand me down clothes, you had to use
You had to make do, you couldn't refuse
This day and age, if you find things hard
Buy now, and pay later, or credit card
A large tin bath, for all to share
If you were last, you didn't care
Not like our baths, with a fancy shower
With running hot water, and electric power
You hand washed clothes, with a board and mangle
No washing machine, where they knot and tangle
On hands and knees you cleaned the floors
No vacuum cleaners to do your chores
With outdoor games children passed the day
No telly's to watch, or computers to play

Went out to work at a very young age
Down the pit to earn a wage
They worked very hard, but loved it so
There were no universities or colleges to go
At night they stayed in, they didn't moan
They had no videos, or mobile phone
No fancy restaurants, or discos at night
Just a night together by candle light
Or if they were lucky, a bulb hung from a wire
No central heating, or instant gas fire
An open coal fire to keep them warm
Or an old heavy coat, all shabby and worn
You hear people say, that those were the days
And now we're so spoilt, in so many ways
We have everything going, all modern and new
Without these facilities, what would we do?
Imagine having nothing, with clothes old and torn
And living on rations, we don't know were born.

TELEVISION

Standing in the corner at the side of the fire
With sockets and scart leads trailing with wire
Facing the chairs where people sit
While reading a paper or even knit
They switch me on and gather around
Through soaps and films there's never a sound
The evening news they love to watch
With a mug of cocoa, or a glass of scotch
Sometimes I'm on for most of the day
To entertain youngsters, while they play
They changed to remote, from knobs on the set
Just shows you how lazy people can get
They should have left them all on the panel
Now people keep flickering from channel to channel
Many a time I'm on for hours
While people are busy, or taking showers
My favourite time that I like best
When they're all in bed and having a rest
Or when they've gone out for more than an hour
I'm all switched off without any power
I have a sleep when I know they've gone
Cos as soon as they're back, they'll switch me on.

THE GNOME

My name is Ronnie, the little gnome
Out in the garden, not far from home
Just by the flowers, plants and shrubs
Where there's lovely pots and garden tubs
And in the corner a bird bath too
A little rabbit out on view
There's birds on the grass, looking for their treat
Beneath the window, a little white seat
Lots of trees, all thick and dense
A little squirrel perched on the fence
Eating the nuts without a care
The birds all anxiously waiting there
It's nice and tranquil, sitting in the sun
But in the winter it's not much fun
Freezing cold with trees all bare
Icicles forming, and snow everywhere
I'm all alone, there's not a sound
Because it's winter no ones around
A little robin, down there I see
Searching for food, he's looking at me
At last I've got a little friend
The rest of winter, together we'll spend.

I'm a little red setter, just sitting there
Outside in a kennel, for people to stare
Sat in a corner all thin and frail
All wet and scruffy with a long thin tail
I see a young couple looking down at me
They're taking me home, how happy I'll be
New collar and lead were on our way
Down to the park to have a play
In my new home I'm looking around
All through the house I leap and bound
Nice shiny bowls for when I'm fed,
And in the corner, a brand new bed
Because of my nature, I like to play
Pinching the washing and running away
They've had their tea; I'm full of go
Digging holes in the garden, they'll never know
I run round the house, there's mud everywhere
Bouncing off walls, and through the air
I've been on my holidays, rite from the start
Wherever they go, we're never apart

Regular walks I always go
But I'm getting old, and a little slow
That doesn't stop me from getting around
I still have my moments, when I leap and bound
Finding old balls at home I keep
Left in the garden all in a heap
I've been very spoilt, and I get my own way
But I know that they've loved me,
from that very first day.

PARACHUTE JUMP

Thousands of feet way up in the sky
Out of a plane I'm going to fly
With parachute on I'm ready to jump
My hearts all pounding, I can feel it thump
Leaping out in the open sky
Watching the plane as it passes by
Gusts of wind pull me everywhere

As I'm floating round in the open air
Down to the ground I'm falling fast
Flocks of birds go flying past
I pull the cord, back up I go
It breaks my fall, I start to flow
Open fields for miles around
As I'm gradually falling nearer the ground
The parachute cord tightly in my hand
I'm in position and ready to land
Hitting the ground on bended knee
The parachute floating just behind me
A sigh of relief, as I sit on the floor
I won't be doing that anymore.

GLOOMY DAY

The weathers gloomy and pouring with rain
I can hear it trickling down the drain
Bouncing off windows, running down in the gutter
A bird in a puddle, his little wings flutter
I'll go for a walk before it gets dark
Down through the field, and around the park
With wellies and coat, umbrella in hand
Off to stroll in the open land
Splashing through puddles as I go by
Brolly out stretched to keep me dry
The grass all squelching and really soggy
Mounds of mud all thick a boggy
My coat soaked right through,
and running down my arm
As I walk with my umbrella, clenched in my palm
The rain still beats down, above my head
I'd much sooner be dry, and tucked up in bed.

Along the canal, we like to walk
Hand in hand, as we laugh and talk
Admiring the boats go sailing by
And baby birds just learning to fly
Two lovely swans, on the path quite near
How sweet and innocent they appear
Approaching a lock, a boats going through
It looks very easy, but hard to do
Down to the bottom, the little boat goes
Watching the water, how fast it flows
We see some ducks just below a ledge
Bobbing about on the waters edge
We're under a tunnel, really long and high
The sound of our echo as we go by
We pass some fishermen, with their catch
Anxiously waiting, they're in a match
There's a little pub, we can see quite near
And people sitting having a beer
With wooden tables, umbrellas too
Overlooking the water, and a beautiful view

A humped back bridge, just closely by
And not a cloud up in the sky
On a bench together we share
In the water the sunlight glare
The ducks are gathering, they're being fed
A lady's throwing them lumps of bread
Were on our return, back home we go
And watching the water, just slowly flow.

THE LONELY
 CHRISTMAS TREE

Decembers the month, my time of year
It's Christmas time when I appear
Standing tall, and all in green
The only time when I am seen
With colored tinsel gleaming bright
And a fancy colored flashing light
Up on top a shining star
And a father Christmas chocolate bar

With lovely baubles all a glow
I'm all dressed up, and out on show
In the window I like to be
Cos people stop and look at me
There's lots of presents, just down below
All neatly wrapped with a lovely bow
Piled up and ready, that's where they'll stay
And can't be opened, till Christmas day
The festive time has come to an end
Twelve months alone again I'll spend
Up in the loft all packed away
Can't wait till next years Christmas day.

~ THE FAIRGROUND ~

The sheer excitement of the fair
The noise and sounds that fill the air
All those colored flashing lights
With stalls and rides, what lovely sights

A roller coaster way up high
And people screaming going by
Those waltzing chairs, how fast they go
Tossing people to and fro
A lovely sound from the carousel
Kids on a roundabout ringing the bell
Passing the ghost train, what an eerie sound
The big wheel spinning round and round
Stalls with darts and balls to toss
Children eating candyfloss
The helter skelter, people love
A laughing policeman up above
The smell of hot-dogs, burgers too
It's fun at the fair, with lots to do
But I'm not keen being swung around
I like my feet safe on the ground.

Every May brean sands we go
To ocean lodge a couple we know
A little site right next to the beach
An open-air pool in easy reach
With miles of sand for the dog to run
While we're sitting bathing in hot blazing sun
An evening stroll to brean down pub
To have a beer, and lovely grub
We watch the sunset starting to fall
And seagulls gather upon the wall
Last year was different, the rain didn't stop
We spent some time in the betting shop
All through the puddles we had to wade
So off to the nearest amusement arcade
On to Weston to spend the day
In pouring rain, where do you stay?
We get some chips for a little treat
Then on to the pier, to find a seat
If only you could have seen us here
Just watching the rain, on Weston pier.

On a cliff top bench, overlooking the sea
In the midday sun, it's the place to be
With a nice café in easy reach
To watch the people on the beach
Boats leave the harbour, for their hourly cruise
Awaiting the speedboat, there's people in queues
Over in the distance, the large castle wall
And just to the right, a big wheel standing tall
Down the sea front, where everyone goes
The arcades and restaurants and late evening shows
Below in the spa, there's crafts and shows too
With a very long bar and plenty to do
In neat little borders, the flowers all grow
And out on the balcony, the chairs in a row
People relaxing, all out for the day
Enjoying the sun and hear the band play
You just can't beat it, and a pleasure to be
Away from it all, overlooking the sea.

In men's old clothes, and frightening mask
Penny for the guy, the children ask
Buying their fireworks you often see
Not thinking how dangerous they can be
But it's so much fun, on bonfire night
With bangers and mash by the fire all bright
Children with sparklers, they anxiously wait
While watching a Catherine wheel, spin on a gate
A rocket from a bottle whizzes into the air
And lights up the sky, like a signalers flare
Jumping Jacks darting, all over the ground
As big roman candles shoot smoke all around
Colored fountains and snowdrops
with sparks all a glow
The sky's full of sparkle what a beautiful show
You can still smell the smoke fumes,
the very next day
And the old burnt out fireworks
and bonfires just lay.

Looking back in the past, at the games we played
Spinning buttons on cotton, the things that we made
French skipping and hopscotch you never see
Two ball and five stones, how happy we'd be
Walking on stilts was the hardest trick
And bouncing around on a pogo stick
Conkers and marbles we had so much fun
Rat a tat ginger and having to run
Out on the field playing rounders all day
It's sad how these days have all gone away.

NEWLY WEDS

Newly weds now husband and wife
Starting together in their new life
Sharing together what the future will bring
Supporting each other with everything
Enjoying each moment they have together
Loving each other for ever and ever.

SON

A son who likes football and climbing trees
Fooling around and scraping your knees
Football shirt and matching shorts
Taking part in all the sports
Whatever you do you do it best
And like to stand out from the rest
Your hopes and dreams your aims are high

Whatever you do you really try
Your determination really shines through
We're here to support you in all you do
You'll always be our number one
Cos you're our very special son.

MEMORIES

If only your face was a picture book
To turn a page and have a look
To see your face and your lovely smile
And reminisce for a little while
The treasured moments we had to share
What would I give to have you there?
I know that this can never be
Those memories will always stay with me
All the time that we're apart
I'll have your picture near my heart.

LITTLE GIRL

A little girl full of fun
Bringing joy to everyone
Nice frilly dresses always so neat
With a cheeky smile looking so sweet
Playing with dolls that brings you pleasure
You're a darling little treasure.

FRIEND

You've been a good friend for the past few years
Had some laughs and shed some tears
Trusting each other the way that you should
Sharing things you know that you could
It's nice to know that someone is there
To take the time and really care
Really nice to have a good friend
To laugh and joke and you can depend.

SOMEONE SPECIAL

Just a few words I'd like to express
To bring you joy and happiness
It's very seldom that you are told
Your full of warmth, with a heart of gold
Always kind to everyone
Smiling cheerful, full of fun
As today's your special day
You're thought of in a special way.

MY LOVE

All my love I send to you
For all those special things you do
The lovely words you often say
Knowing you're there at night and day
Treasuring each moment we have to share
Just knowing how much you really care

It doesn't seem long since our wedding day
And said love, honor, and obey
After all these years you melt my heart
And hope we never, ever part.

BOTH OF YOU

Very best wishes to both of you
Wishing you luck in all you do
Fulfilling your hopes and dreams in life
Without any struggles, sorrow or strife
Enjoying your lives without any fears
Having many pleasurable wonderful years.

MUM

Lovely words can mean so much
A bunch of flowers gives an added touch
Thinking of you on this special day
That lots of happiness comes your way
Feelings for you we rarely show
Your loved more than you'll ever know.

GRANDAD

Grandad is a special man
Sits and chats whenever he can
His gentle nature and lovely ways
Telling you stories of bygone days
He takes an interest in all you do
Asking questions and helping you
Always they're since the day of my birth
You're the best grandad on this earth.

NAN

Nan's are loving with a very kind heart
With our upbringing you like to take part
Loving ways with a gentle touch
Supportive and willing nothing too much
Always there for babysitting
Making things that you enjoy knitting
You're thought of in every special way
And mean more than any words can say.

WISHES

Special wishes just for you
For all your kindness and things you do
The time you spend and show you care
Thinking of others and always there
Your loving ways and added touch
All these things, they mean so much.

Special words especially for you
To thank you for all the things you do
Your caring smile, your gentle touch
Shows you're loving and care so much
Always there to lend a hand
And knows exactly where you stand
Your greatly appreciated in every way
Remembered and thought of every day.

THE ZOO

The kind of animals you see in the zoo
All different species, and things they do
Monkeys and chimps, the children they tease
While apes just sit there looking for fleas
Lions and tigers they love to roar
In the next cage, a great wild boar
Sitting doing nothing he likes to stare
Over by the water stands a white polar bear

With his baby close by and looking so proud
The sound of a hyena laughing out loud
Lovely flamingo's a beautiful pink
And skunks that give off, a terrible stink
A toucan who'd give you a nasty peck
An elegant giraffe with his lovely long neck
Black panthers marching up and down
Hippos looking with a solemn frown
Zebra's taking it, all in their stride
As a crocodile lays, with his mouth open wide
Elephants enjoying their daily bath
As penguins waddle across the path
Panda's with their lovely black eyes
Getting annoyed with the hovering flies
There's many more animals I'm sure you'll find
They're interesting to watch, and they won't mind.

Sitting outside in the evening air
A lovely night together we share
Looking up at the beautiful evening sky
Watching the clouds go floating by
All shapes and sizes, colours too
And just behind the sky all blue
We see a plane in the evening light
So far away and gleaming bright
A long white trail it leaves behind
The planes flown by, and hard to find
Staring up at the moon, all bright and clear
Watching the stars as they appear
It's getting dark now, nightfall it will be
And birds still singing in the tree
The clouds have gone, the sky is vast
A shooting star goes flying past
It's peaceful sitting just us pair
All lovely and tranquil, without a care.

THE GREAT
CENTRAL WALK

The great central walk an old railway line
A beautiful walk when the weather is fine
Just me and the dog alone for a walk
All peaceful and quiet not having to talk
Looking over the countryside what a beautiful view
With cows in the fields and rabbits too
A lovely stroll in the evening sun
The dog all inquisitive and having fun
Trees and bushes, there all around
It's really tranquil and not a sound
Only the birds singing up in the tree
Not a soul around, just the dog and me
Walking under the bridge, there's steps to the farm
Another nice walk, all peaceful and calm
I'm approaching a stream, all lovely and clear
What can I say; it's beautiful here
There's a little bench not far away
To sit and pass the time of day
A sudden coolness from the evening breeze
And the sound of rustling through the trees

There's a mass of thistles and lots of clover
I'm on my return my walk is over.

CHILDREN'S PARTIES

Children's parties full of joy
Fun for every girl and boy
Girls dressed up in pretty frocks
With matching shoes and fancy socks
Boys all smart and hair in place
Shiny shoes you can see your face
The tables laid, it's time to eat
They're all excited as they take a seat
Assorted sandwiches with chicken dips
Sausages, cheese and potato chips
Then comes the ice cream and strawberry jelly
Which drops on the floor and flicks on the telly
With cake on their face, and jam down their dress
Those lovely clean clothes, "oh what a mess "

It's time for the games, chasing balloons everywhere
Knocking down ornaments, toppling over a chair
Follows pass the parcel then blind mans buff
Musical chairs, and all that stuff
Times getting on, it's just turned five
Parties now over, parents arrive
Whatever happened to that lovely clean child?
Now looking all dirty, untidy and wild.

MOTORWAYS

It's always busy on a motorway
No matter what time it is, night or day
Traveling along at a steady speed
There's always someone taking the lead
Always racing to get there fast
You often see them flying past
Showing off, the fancy car they own
While chatting on, their mobile phone
Lorries pulling out, cos they won't wait

They've got their deliveries, and can't be late
Caravans being towed, they're going away
For a long weekend, or a holiday
Broken down vehicles on the hard shoulder you find
Cyclists with motorbikes, taking time to unwind
People always hogging the middle lane
Someone flashes them over, they try in vain
But whether your journey is short or long
It's the best way of traveling, if nothing goes wrong
There's always the incidents and road works too
Which causes delays, and a great traffic queue
Then people's patients, and tempers flair
If you weren't in a hurry, you just wouldn't care.

I'd love to be an astronaut, walking on Mars
Where there's no busy traffic, lorries and cars
Looking out at the stars so far away
Not knowing what time it is night or day
I won't be alone, with friends I'll be
With places to go, and things to see
We're off exploring this wonderful place
Millions of miles way out in space
The grounds all hard, and really dry
On this planet, way up in the sky
There's not a soul and not a sound
Only the stars from miles around
No sign of life here can be found
Is there anyone else around?
The time has come, we have to go
We're so disheartened, we'll both never know.

SUMMER

Clocks put forward summer's begun
Those lovely days of beautiful sun
No need for fires and nice hot stews
It's garden parties and barbecues
Lovely flowers all out on show
The grass keeps growing and needs a mow
Hanging baskets with flowers all bright
Nice long nights of evening light
Leaves on trees all types and shades
Birds on branches with nests they've made
The time of year for wasps and bees
Moths and ants and little grass fleas
Days when it's clammy and really warm
Follows the showers and a thunderstorm
Summer has passed the nights draw nigh
Autumn's upon us, doesn't time fly.

A drop in temperature and morning dew
No more warmth and skies all blue
With gusty winds and feeling cold
And autumn leaves a lovely gold
Broken branches all around
Leaves all scattered on the ground
Acorns falling off the trees
No sign of any wasps or bees
The grass has stopped growing
The flowers have died
It's looking quite bare in the countryside
No more animals out to graze
The fields all soil, no bright yellow maize
Just a lonely scarecrow in a field all-bare
With nothing around, and no birds to scare
Halloween's approaching and bonfire night
Candles in pumpkins and sparklers all bright
Clocks go back as winter is near
Shops filling up with festive cheer
Decorations on trees and Santa on sleigh
It won't be long for Christmas day.